HOW I BEAT SELF SABOTAGE
AND HOW YOU CAN TOO

by
Erica Snyder

ISBN 978-0-9894219-1-1
©2013 Gypsy Publishing
Printed in the USA
ericasnyder.com

ACKNOWLEDGEMENTS

This book would not be possible without the love and support of my husband. It has been a long and surprisingly therapeutic journey. Your patience has been a gift. I also want to thank my parents, my brother, and my aunt. Thank you for listening. I'd like to thank the close friends that I'm so blessed to have in my life right now and all of the past friends who've touched me along the way. Finally, I want to thank all of you who are about to read this book. I hope you know how much you mean to me... I truly hope that you will take something away from this book that will help you in some small way.

PREFACE

Seven years ago I was hung over, lethargic, pre-diabetic, obese, directionless, and depressed. The month before my dream wedding I was trying on wedding dresses, 50 pounds overweight. With my whole life in front of me all I wanted to do was crawl into a hole and die. Then I became sick and tired of being sick and tired and decided to change my life. It seemed easy on paper. Just buckle down and make some changes - lose weight - get healthy - start pursuing my goals and dreams. But no matter how sincere my intention, and no matter how hard I tried, I found it very difficult to even get started. When I did, I just kept quitting. Through a lot of soul searching I eventually discovered that self sabotage was the one thing that kept showing up whenever I decided to pursue any kind of positive change in my life. In order to start living the life that I'd always dreamed for myself it became my mission to beat self sabotage. I became obsessed with learning all I could about it.

After a lot of time spent searching I discovered that while there was no shortage of scientific data about self sabotage out there, and certainly no shortage of ineffective remedies being offered to manage self sabotage, there was a serious lack of any meaningful, simple, real life, real world, impactful solutions available to beat it. So through a lot of trial and error, countless false starts, and a lot of frustration, I discovered, adapted and applied several different strategies that not only helped me manage the feelings and emotions that accompany self sabotage, but beat it altogether. I'm not saying it's not a struggle, some times daily, but I beat self sabotage and I know you can too.

When I set out to write this book I knew I wasn't a professional writer. I knew there would likely be sentence structure issues, grammatical errors, and probably a few past tense/present tense arguments in a sentence here or there. But all of that didn't matter. The important thing for me is to share with you, as best I can, a few of the most impactful strategies and exercises that have helped me change my life, and I believe will help you too. My wish is for you to beat self sabotage and to start living the life you were meant to live.

I'd like to ask you for a favor before you start reading this book. Take your time. One of the drums that I seem to be beating more and more these days is of slowing down. The pace of this world drives me crazy sometimes. We live in a microwave it, instant message it, hurry it up world. It seems like we are trying to get through whatever we're doing faster and faster so we can quickly get on to the next thing.

As you embark on your journey of beating self sabotage it's important to take your time. As you read through this book, take your time. There is no doubt you could get through it in one or two sittings, but it's not a race. My husband and I are reading Tao De Ching and we regularly get hung up for weeks contemplating just one page of that book, sometimes just one sentence. So the favor I ask of you is to please take your time. Some of the methods and exercises in this book might seem a little hokey. No one is looking though and you're worth it. Take your time and enjoy the journey of life.

There are wealth's of joy in some of the smallest things that we pass by at break neck speeds throughout the day. Thank you for taking the time to share this one with me...

INTRODUCTION

INTRODUCTION

Self sabotage shows up in our lives in one form or another every single day. How we react to thoughts and emotions that accompany self sabotage is the real determining factor of how things will turn out in any given situation. Life is coming at us at a dizzying pace each day - home, job, relationships, bills, information, technology, traffic, fitness, meals, kids... the list goes on and on. Daily pressures are endless and it only seems to be getting worse. It seems there isn't enough time in the day to accomplish even half of what we need to accomplish anymore. The modern American life is perfectly engineered to produce a constant stream of moments throughout each day in which to engage in self sabotaging thoughts.

Guilt - fear - doubt - procrastination. To one degree or another we've all suffered the effects of self sabotage at some point in our lives, whether we were aware of it or not. Perhaps we missed out on a job opportunity, got caught in a cycle of yo-yo dieting, or maybe we've suffered the ending of an important relationship. Whatever the effect, our reaction to self sabotaging thoughts has likely changed the course of our life... forever. But before we all slide off the deep end over-thinking that, let me offer this; the absolute perfection of life is that the moment we open our eyes each morning we are presented with a clean slate, a total reset, a fresh opportunity to start anew. The realization of our biggest goals and our wildest dreams is never much further than a moment away...

So what is self sabotage? Why should I care? Scientists and psychologists have filled volumes outlining varying definitions and offering brilliant explanations of what self sabotage is and the theories behind it. But in the spirit of keeping it real and getting to the point please pay very close attention to the following simple definition; self sabotage is a behavior, often in the form of an inner monologue, that ultimately interferes with goals and dreams. The key word to hone in on in here is *interferes*. Self sabotage doesn't have the power on its own to eliminate or erase our goals and dreams. It only interferes with our reaching them. That's an awesome thought if you think about it because the power to reach our goals and realize our dreams is truly, solely ours.

So why should you care about all of this? Consider the following - self sabotage is the primary driving force and root cause preventing us from reaching our goals or realizing our dreams. This is huge! The negative effects of self sabotage are crippling, life altering even. Believe me, I've lived with self sabotage and felt its negative effects most of my life. When the clouds began to finally clear away, and strategies for beating my own self sabotaging behavior were put into practice, everything in my life changed for the better! When the fog lifted I was finally able to stop looking at myself through the veil of self sabotaging thoughts and behaviors and start honestly seeing my true self. I emerged energized and became motivated to really start living, to experiencing life fully, and to stop wasting time focusing on fears and doubts and debilitating guilt.

It didn't happen overnight. In my quest to overcome self sabotage there were more than a few false starts. While I was able to identify self sabotage as the root cause of my living in reaction to fear and doubt and guilt, I hadn't yet discovered effective solutions for managing self sabotage and eradicating it from my life. It took wasting some time working through a lot of flat, ineffective approaches that only put a band aid on the problem, to eventually discover several very effective strategies for actually *beating* self sabotage once and for all. Once I really started to feel the positive effects eradicating self sabotaging behaviors had in my life I became very passionate about helping others beat this monster too. I wanted to share the discoveries I made for removing the filter of fear, doubt and guilt that you might be seeing yourself through to reveal the you you really are so you might live fully and achieve your goals and your dreams. This is my motivation for writing this book.

Whether your goals are fitness or wellness related, if you want to start a new business or go back to school, or maybe you want to change careers, move across country or move across the world - whatever your goals or dreams might be - whether the changes you seek or the visions you see for yourself are big or small, and you feel like there's something preventing you from taking meaningful steps towards it, more than likely the block your feeling is rooted in self sabotage. I'd like to help you get out of your own way, throw a little caution to the wind, and start living the life you were meant to live!

THE BACK STORY

THE BACK STORY

Anyone who knows me will tell you that I am my least favorite subject. But to put a little perspective on how or why self sabotage became a part of my life I wanted to share just a little bit about my back story. Needless to say, this chapter will be kept short and sweet.

We all have unique life stories. The cosmos have produced an endless array of life events that have led us all to the unique places where we find ourselves today. My story is probably very similar to yours. I grew up in the Midwest. My parents were old school. I love and respect my parents deeply and am so thankful for them. I'm much more thankful for them now than I was when I was growing up though. They were hardworking and fiercely loyal to family and church. After over 30 years of marriage they divorced. I was 19. My dad passed away a little over a year ago. My brother, who's always been one of my heroes, is eight years

older than me. We were very close, but because of
our age difference we lived in totally separate
worlds throughout my childhood. As I was starting
the 5th grade, my brother was moving into a college
dorm. So, for the most part, I spent my childhood
alone.

Whether it was because of the typical ways of the
Bible belt culture in the Midwest, or because I was
the younger sibling and my parents had already
"been there and done that" with my older brother, or
maybe because of some generationally rooted
family ideology - whatever the reason a deep sense
of fear and doubt was instilled in me from a very
early age. The strategy used to keep me close and to
keep me safe from the world was to make me so
afraid of it that I wouldn't dare want to venture a
closer look. That story could fill volumes by itself.
But even with as much havoc that was unwittingly
wreaked in my life, in many ways I was my own
worst enemy. Knowing what I knew and seeing
what I saw throughout my family growing up -

alcoholism, fear, guilt and self destruction - I still chose to travel a path in a mad search for my own perfect trifecta of self destruction - abusing alcohol, abusing drugs, and becoming dangerously obese. Whether it was food or intoxicants it seemed I couldn't numb myself enough to the madness around me. Secretly I yearned for something more. My immediate dream was to not just be as geographically far away as possible but I also dreamed about being healthy and fit and free from all of the alcohol induced "so called" fun I couldn't stop having.

When it came to pursuing dreams, or even school assignments, chores, or most anything at all, procrastination was a favorite diversionary tactic of mine. When it came to making any kind of positive change, or even when it came to tackling little, every day tasks like dishes, or paying bills, or getting a school or work project done, tomorrow always seemed like a much better time to do it than today. Procrastination is a tricky form of self sabotage. Being fit and living a healthy lifestyle was something I always yearned for, but I took every opportunity to make terrible food choices and party all the time... My excuse was that I was young. I'm supposed to be having fun now. I'd rather fit in than be fit... I'll be healthy later. Despite an inner desire to live healthier, to pursue my quest for fitness and wellness, or to just be the me I knew I could be, I couldn't manage to get out of my own way. I was surrounded by negativity and I was feeding into most of it. Nobody around me talked much about a future that was very exciting to them so I couldn't grasp a very exciting future for myself either. Deep down I wanted something more, but it seemed like a world away. It was much easier to just go along with the group. Besides, there was always tomorrow to make a change...

Sometimes it takes something drastic to shock us into coherence. For me, it was my annual physical one year. Like so many before I thought I could just show up, jump through some hoops, get my clean bill of health, and go about my merry way. But this time, my doctor had something slightly different to report. With a very sober look she informed me that the sedentary lifestyle I was living, the bad food choices, nicotine and alcohol consumption, was starting to catch up with me. Adverse health effects were starting to show up. My blood pressure was high, my cholesterol was high and I was pre-diabetic. But I was only 25... she must be looking at the wrong chart. She then used words that nearly gave me a heart attack right then and there. "Erica, you are approaching morbid obesity." Morbid obesity! How could this be? Again, I thought she must have the wrong chart in front of her because she couldn't possibly be talking about me, right? Wrong.

My doctor literally gave me orders that day to clean up my lifestyle and lose weight or else face the consequences.

So I had high blood pressure, I was a pre-diabetic, I was borderline morbidly obese and I was only 25.

On top of all of this, I was about to get married. It was time for a change and tomorrow wasn't an option anymore.

At this point, all the excuses in the world weren't going to change the fact that I needed to act, and act quickly. I felt I had no choice. Sometimes that's a good place to be. Sometimes we are forced to get out of our own way. With our back up against the wall we either fight or fall. I decided to get mad and fight. And a fight I knew it would be. I knew there wasn't a magic pill and I knew it wasn't going to be easy.

10 MINUTES

10 MINUTES

It was May 2007, and in less than a month I was leaving for a 10-day trip to Hawaii for my wedding. Motivated by the daunting news I had just received from my doctor, and also by this weird notion of not keeling over before my first wedding anniversary, I knew I had no choice but to make a bold move towards getting myself healthy. But how? I wasn't about to step foot in a gym full of pretty, fit people in the shape that I was in. It was then when I remembered this annoyingly persistent infomercial for a home fitness DVD program I always tried to quickly click through as I was laying on the couch, watching TV, eating some god-awful thing at night. The program looked really hard, maybe too hard for me to do....so I ordered it. Thinking back, this may have been another one of my clever, preemptive self sabotaging maneuvers. I probably visualized myself trying it for 5 or 10 minutes and saying, "well I tried honey but it was just too hard" so I'd have an excuse to quit. Anyway, we left for Hawaii, had an amazing wedding and an amazing time. When we returned, much to my dismay, there was this little brown box inside of our front door that had been delivered while we were gone. Coming off the excitement of the whirlwind trip we'd just been on I was too tired to think about it, but knew the time had come to finally make a change. The gauntlet had been dropped. I drew a line in the sand and decided I was going to just try my best and damn the consequences!

Having had some previous experience with training and nutrition my husband put together a meal plan for me and the next morning, with laptop and DVD in tow, I hit the basement with a vengeance. Looking back now I have to laugh. That first week, I could only do *a* pushup, and even that was a challenge. My initial goal of twenty minutes on the treadmill started out as three. I thought I was going to die in those three minutes! Often I thought I'd quit. But thankfully, I applied some really good advice I'd just used to stop smoking. "Just take it ten minutes at a time. All you have to do is make it through the next ten minutes. Focus on just those ten minutes." Great advice because at first my cardio and weightlifting routine combined only lasted ten minutes... including breaks! But I stuck with it, laser focused, ten minutes at a time.

With the DVD came access to a pretty active on line forum full of people just like me I felt I could cry to when I needed to. This was incredibly helpful. Between the support I felt from the virtual community, and from my husband and other family, plus knowing I only had to make it through the next ten minutes, I actually started to see progress. My ten minute workouts became fifteen, then twenty, and it wasn't too long until I found myself completing the entire workout - start to finish - including 45-minutes of cardio.

While I didn't see much difference visually right away, I felt better than I had for years. So I stuck with it - ten minutes at a time. It was painful. Very painful. I wanted to quit every single day. I kept telling myself that it would get easier, and it did. My husband took pictures of me on day one. Front view, back view, left view, right view -YIKES! On day 30, I have to admit I didn't feel like I could really see very much improvement in the mirror, but when we put the 30-day pictures side by side with my day one pictures I was shocked to actually see a slightly smaller me. From there I was hooked. That was all the motivation I needed. Not only was I feeling great but now I could actually see the fruits of my labor paying off in those pictures. Day 60 pictures next to day 30 pictures were another great surprise and by the time I had completed my initial goal of 90 days, I was literally a totally different person. At this point in my journey I had lost a whopping 35 pounds of fat, had gained 5 pounds of muscle, and had lost six inches from around my waist. The surprises kept coming...

Part of the online forum I had been participating in over the past 90 days was an invitation to post progress pictures. Each month the company who sponsored the site gave away prizes, including a top prize of $10,000 for the best weight loss transformations. Despite the embarrassment of my day one photos - messed up hair and being in my bra and underwear - my husband encouraged me to enter my photos anyway. Not too long after entering I was actually chosen as the top transformation winner! I couldn't believe it. And if this weren't enough, not long after winning the top transformation contest, I was invited on an all expense paid trip to California to be featured in one of their national TV infomercials - just like the one I had tried so hard to avoid watching months before... The whole thing was amazing. And to think just a few short months prior, I was clinically obese. I could hardly wait to see my doctor again. I'd soon have the chance.

Several months later the time came for my annual doctor visit again and by this time I had lost a total of 50 pounds. I'd gone from a size 16 to a size 4. I was looking so forward to walking into that office and showing her the new me. I'd made her a promise the year before that I was going to follow her advice and when I walked in to her office, she didn't even recognize me. My own doctor didn't recognize me! She had to take a seat when she realized who I was. It was amazing.

Later, one of our close friends we hadn't seen in a while stopped by to visit. He didn't recognize me either. He later told my husband he thought I was my little sister... and I don't have a little sister! It's still one of the best compliments I've ever received.

MAGIC MONDAY

MAGIC MONDAY

We all know the definition of insanity is doing the same thing over and over and expecting a different result. So why do we do it? When it comes to setting and pursuing goals, or realizing dreams, the objective is to overcome obstacles standing in our way. So why is it then that *we* become our biggest obstacle? We take the time to come up with brilliant ideas for our lives, and we have the most sincere intent to realize our dreams, but then we engineer circumstances that derail the very success we seek before we even give ourselves a chance to get started. We're pretty clever about it too. We get very good at setting traps and at constructing minefields in our pathways ensuring we will never reach our intended destination. Exerting great amounts of energy we set ourselves up for failure. One of the more subtle ways we do this is with what I call Magic Monday's.

When it comes to health and fitness we admire the bodies of the models and athletes we see in magazines or on TV. We visualize ourselves achieving *that* body. With a lot of conviction we decide we're going to do whatever it takes to get there. We make our plans, we buy new exercise clothes, fitness DVD's, organize our schedules and formulate perfect strategies of attack. We're convinced! We can do this thing. All we have to do is follow the plan, get over the hump, turn it into a habit, a lifestyle, and then we'll be in the clear. That body will be ours! We then pick a day to draw a line in the sand and start our new life, as the new us.

Monday is almost always the magic day. "It's all going to change starting Monday!" Usually by Wednesday though a totally different conversation starts taking place in our heads. *"Why did I sign up for this? This is so stupid - who does this! You know, I actually like my body, those people in magazines don't even look healthy, they're probably not happy either; they're all photoshopped anyway.... Oh forget it, I'm going to the bar after work... I really love their fries!"* And the cycle continues. I've been there a hundred times myself. Often by the very next Monday we're back to the "I can do this!" conversation in our head again, making plans to start our new life the following Monday. Isn't it great how we always set our goals to start on Monday so we don't interrupt our weekends? I love that. Don't mess with my weekends!

By the way, it's not just ambitions of losing weight either. "Magic Monday's" bring the promise of new us's on many fronts. One of my old favorites used to be "Monday I'm going to quit smoking." I usually threw away a perfectly good pack of cigarettes on Sunday night. By Monday afternoon, I'd totally lost my cool and was fiending so bad that I had to make a bee line to the store to buy another pack. I wonder how much money I wasted doing that... And drinking! Oh my goodness, how many times did I swear off drinking. "Starting Monday I'm going to stop drinking - and stop smoking - and become a vegetarian - and get into pro athlete shape

- and...." It's crazy the pressures we put on ourselves! I have to admit though, once I picked a magic Monday to quit drinking, I had so much fun the weekend before. After all this was the "last weekend I would drink," might as well make it a blow out.

So what is it? We have these great goals. We say them out loud, bring in accountability partners, share them with our friends and family - *we do all the right things* -but somehow, we end up heading in the opposite direction of where we set out to go. By now you're probably saying to yourself, "Erica! What do Monday's have to do with any of this!" O.k. here it is. The thing about change, about creating new habits in life in order to reach a goal or realize a dream, is you have to want it - *really* want it. If your perfectly laid out plan for change includes a scheduling conflict before you even get started, (i.e. I'll start this perfect plan on Monday because the girls have that thing this weekend and I'm looking forward to the dinner with so and so and I really want to enjoy one last whatever") you probably don't *really* want it all that bad in the first place. Monday is one of the traps we subconsciously set for ourselves, one of those land mines we strategically place in our pathway. I've been there more times than I care to mention. I wasn't free from the bondage that Magic Monday's created for me until I took an honest look in the mirror, and then followed a couple important steps.

The very first and most important step to take to beat the curse of Magic Monday is to forget about a start day for your great new plan for change. Start now - right this second. I know an Olympic marathon coach who's trained the most elite, professional athletes in the world. She said that the magic of elite athletes is their ability to train in a mental place that exists in a realm above everyone else - and I don't mean from a superiority perspective. There is a realm of focus and commitment that lays outside the acceptance of the drudgery day to day brings. A place where these athletes choose to go in order to accomplish whatever it is they're trying to accomplish. Everyone has the ability to go there. And for a period of time, early in the journey of your quest for change, you have to decide to go there. This doesn't mean you abandon friends or activities, per se. It just means you have to decide that the lifelong benefits of achieving the goal or dream you're seeking is more important than the three minute thrill of a sugar buzz, or a nicotine buzz, or even a negative conversation. For me, there were deep fears and feelings of guilt that led me to believe I just didn't deserve my dreams. I would go through the motions of making a perfect plan, because this is what we do, but there was a little voice deep down inside telling me I really don't have what it takes to succeed in the first place. I believed those feelings of fear and guilt more than I believed I could actually reach my goals and realize success. The Magic Monday was just a diversion of sorts. A temporary, feel good tactic. You feel good about making the plans. You're sincere. You're serious.

But the fact that you're already putting it off is a tell tale sign that you're setting those traps and placing those land mines that will prevent you from making it through the week, let alone all the way to your goal. You have to decide your vision is bigger than your fears, bigger than your doubts, bigger than even you are. Decide that *this* minute is *the* minute when it all changes. Don't wait until Monday.

The next step I had to take was a little tough. But after the sheer frustration of cycling through countless Magic Monday's, I had to physically look at myself in the mirror, right in the eyes, and just plain confess that I was being lazy. We all want the benefits of positive change but we often fail to consider the work involved. Sometimes really hard work. When I started on my journey of change I was fifty pounds overweight, so the first thing I had to do was climb a giant mountain. There were many times when I realized it was easier for me to go along with the feelings of fear and guilt I was having, and to use them as a crutch to avoid the hard work of taking steps towards reaching my goals.

Admitting to myself I was basically being a lazy slug wasn't easy. Accepting responsibility for my own actions was a critical step for me to take early in this process though.

Fear and guilt breed doubt - doubt leads to inaction - inaction is the wall standing between us, and the life we were meant to live.

BURNING BOWL

BURNING BOWL

People are cruel to each other in this world. Kids in particular can be so cruel. But in my experience people are equally as cruel to themselves as they are to others, maybe even more so. Over the years I've had the awesome opportunity to teach, coach and train countless people and the magnitude of cruelty I've seen people level against themselves never ceases to amaze me.

The ways in which we treat ourselves badly are endless. In many ways, it's an expected practice of the modern American experience to purposely put ourselves in the line of fire. Consider the typical day for the typical person in anywhere USA. The day usually starts with self induced sleep deprivation, followed by a steady stream of self induced malnutrition throughout the day, and then ends with self induced chronic stress brought on by relationship pressures, money pressures, work performance pressures, traffic pressures and pressures that persist from the knowledge that tomorrow will likely be a similar repeat of today. One of the worst ways we display cruelty to ourselves is through feelings of guilt. Usually these feelings are unsubstantiated, but for whatever reason we humans feel guilty about most everything. What we eat, how we look, what we do, what we don't do, what we think about, the state of the world, original sin, what he said, what she said. Guilt is a breeding ground for worry. As kooky as this seems, there are more than a few family members of mine who have literally worried themselves to death.

Incidentally, in Tibet, or more specifically in Tibetan, a word for guilt doesn't exist. The Tibetan culture has no understanding of the kind of social guilt we experience on a daily basis. The closest related word can be translated as *"an intelligent regret that decides to do things differently."*

Anyway, some time ago I discovered an exercise for letting go of guilt, as well as fear, doubt and anything else you can imagine one may need to rid themselves of. The exercise is called the burning bowl. I performed the burning bowl ceremony during my journey of beating self sabotage and it actually had more of an effect on me than I thought it would. The burning bowl is nothing new. There are many cultures, churches, healing centers, new age groups and people of all walks of life who practice the ceremony. In my research though I discovered that most ceremonies involve a group of people, and it usually occurs within the time constraints of an organized or scheduled service. This is all well and good. I'm certain that these participants were all well served. But I believe that in order to experience the fullness of the burning bowl ceremony there should be no time constraints in preparing to perform it, and it should be experienced alone.

Some may consider the burning bowl ceremony a little quirky. Some may think it's a little too symbolic, offering no real long-term effect. But if you truly immerse yourself in it, let go, and allow the magic in, believe in it - meditatively and honestly - it will have dramatic, long lasting effects. Please try. This is an important step on the road to beating self sabotage.

To prepare for the burning bowl ceremony, sit quietly in a quiet, private space and write down words or short phrases representing every fear, every doubt and every sense of guilt you're feeling. Write the words out big enough so only 10 or 15 words fit on a letter size piece of paper. You may only use one piece of paper or you may fill an entire tablet. Whatever the case, just take your time and get it all out. This process may happen in one sitting and it may take several. It doesn't matter. Hold nothing back and write every word you feel come up in your spirit. Meditate on your life, take an honest assessment and write down pains you've felt, pains you've caused, write out words describing actions or events that cause you to feel fear, doubt, shame, guilt, worry, etc... Write out names... Let yourself go, give yourself the freedom to lay it all out on paper. This is for your eyes only.

So there they are. All of the words that represent all of your deepest darkest fears and doubts and guilt's and pains have been written down. There they are before you. Take a minute to see all of them together, out in the light, like a group of hooligans that live to do nothing more than torment you. Every single word has been attached to you in some way. They've become comfortable being part of you, clinging to you for life, feeding off you and feeding off of each other - strengthening over time. Some words have been with you for so long you've hardly noticed they were there anymore. When they first took up residence, they weren't welcome, it was uncomfortable, but now they've just become part of the landscape around you. Frankly, there are some words you feel a level of comfort in. Like the effects of the Stockholm syndrome - they've held you captive for so long you've grown to like them, befriend them, even protect them.

It's time to let them go.

With scissors, cut each word out so it's on its own individual piece of paper. If you'll allow it, this part of the ceremony can be impactful by itself - kind of setting the tone. Quiet your mind and see each word as just a word on a piece of paper now. Without other words to feed off, and without you to give them life, they start to lose their strength.

Visualize each word as separate from yourself now. They are no longer part of you. Allow yourself to start to feel the strength each word held over you diminish - like they're being removed from the life source that's been feeding them, keeping them alive, and empowering them for so long.
Now it's time to perform the final step in the burning bowl ceremony. Put each individual piece

of paper, each word, someplace safe - like in a stainless steel bowl or in a fireplace. Say goodbye to these words forever and set the paper on fire. Watch the flame spread from one piece of paper to the other. Watch each paper curl up in flames, turn to ash, and disappear. If the flames go out, light the remaining pieces of paper until every piece has been consumed with flames and reduced to ash. Allow yourself to physically feel all of those negative emotions that have held you captive leave your presence and drift away forever on the clouds of smoke that rise up.

Meditate on this experience, take note of what you're feeling and visualize yourself totally liberated, free and unencumbered. It's important to take this experience into your spirit so you can remember it and recall it often. When I did this ceremony I recalled the memory and feeling of liberation several times a day for months afterwards in order to form new habits. I wanted to remind

myself to not go back, to not let those emotions
back into my life. They weren't welcome anymore...

THE CIRCLE

THE CIRCLE

It has been my experience that unless our aspirations closely resemble the aspirations of the people in our everyday lives, those people will often assist us in self sabotaging our goals and dreams.

Dreams are fragile things and dreamers are even more fragile. We dreamers are already struggling through our own fears and doubts to even get to a place where we can share them with others out loud. This is fertile ground for self sabotage. Toss in a disparaging comment or two from a trusted friend, family member or, worse yet, someone we really look up to and admire, and it doesn't take much for self sabotage to grab hold of us and completely derail our dreams.

It happens all the time, especially if our goals and dreams are big and scary, or out of the ordinary. Well meaning (or maybe not to so well meaning) people in our lives tend to offer us input and advice that ends up feeding right into the self sabotaging fears and doubts we are battling to avoid. The problem is, most people are usually drudging out an existence they wish they could change somehow. Most don't have the courage though. So if we muster up the courage to not only dream a big dream, but to share it with others, they won't want you to beat them to happiness. They won't want you to leave them behind. So they'll lay down a clever trail of comments and suggestions designed to subliminally illustrate why you're crazy for having such silly dreams in the first place. And we buy into it, often leaving our dreams on the shelf for another day. Pretty soon day's turn into months, another year goes by, and eventually, dreams are forgotten altogether.

For years I kept my goals and dreams and ambitions under wraps for fear of what people would think or say. The longer I hid them, the more I started buying into those fears... until one day, I'd had enough. Remember the burning bowl? For me, the circle exercise became a perfect companion to the burning bowl. After all, I'd just purged all of the negative emotions I'd been carrying around with me for years. I surely didn't want them to find their way back in, and I knew they'd try.

The circle, like the burning bowl, isn't a new concept. And also like the burning bowl the circle can seem a little quirky and flat. But it's critically important to give this exercise some serious dimension though and allow it to really become part of your DNA. In order to do that, I learned early to keep the circle front and center in my life, every day, until it took a firm hold - until it became a habit. I have to admit, I love the circle. It's sort of an excuse to be a hard nose when you have to be. It's empowering and freeing. The feelings of liberation I experienced during the burning bowl ceremony were amplified with the circle. The circle simplifies how you deal with day-to-day decision making in your life.

Here's how it works. 1. Take a blank piece of paper and draw a stick figure inside a circle. The stick figure represents you, alone and content, inside an empty circle. No fear, no doubt, no guilt. Nothing. Just you. 2. Also inside the circle, write out your dreams, your goals, and whatever visions you have for your life. Write them in succinct words or phrases. 3. Outside the circle, write out all of the words and short phrases that represent the negative thoughts you may be having yourself about reaching your goals. Also write out not so supportive comments you get, or feel like you might get, from the people in your life when you share your dreams. Lastly, write down any words or phrases from everyday life you feel might throw you off track in any way.

Immediately seeing this visual illustration - *me and*
my goals and dreams inside a safe, impenetrable
circle separate from all of the negative influences of
the world around me - was somewhat of an eye

51

opener in and of itself. It helped me to see that I was in control of what I allowed inside my circle and where I placed the power. Why should outside negative forces be given any focus, any energy or any power to determine whether or not I pursue my goals and dreams?

Just because a trusted friend, family member or advisor presents you with an opinion or commentary about your dreams doesn't make the opinion or commentary right, no matter who it comes from. You still have the power to accept or reject it if you choose. If it's good for you, if it supports you and your goals, allow it inside the circle. If it doesn't, don't. Period. This doesn't mean you reject that person, just the presentation of their opinion or commentary as it relates to your goals and dreams.

The circle has become part of my every day life. I don't leave home without it, so to speak. Wherever I may be at any given time, if I don't physically have a circle of some kind on me I will look around and locate something round nearby to serve as a reminder of the circle. No matter where I am in the world and no matter what I'm doing at any given moment there will be a circle of some kind within reach or within view to serve as a constant reminder of *my* sacred circle. It's forced me to form new habits, which is one of the most important ingredients for beating self sabotage. There are just a very few things allowed inside my sacred circle anymore.

This exercise isn't meant to make you rigid, guarded or jaded. It's meant to be a reminder that you are in the drivers seat when it comes to your life and your goals and your dreams. In fact, go through your days completely open to all of the possibilities around you. Be welcoming of all ideas, all people and all influences surrounding you. There is much to be learned with an open mind, an open heart, and with open eyes. But be sure to remember that ideas and influences presented to you are just that, presentations. There isn't a rule that says you have to decide the merits of any presentation the instant it's given. Take it under advisement, not as gospel, and only allow things inside your circle that support and nourish you.

The circle applies to everyday life as well. When life happens, a car cuts you off on the road, negative or unsupportive conversations are going on around you, the boss is being a jerk, drama at work - whatever it is - these things are just presentations of an idea or a thought or a feeling. You have the choice whether or not to let them inside your circle, i.e. your life. You have to make this exercise cut and dry. No exceptions. No guilt. No regret. It's not always easy. There have been many times when I've rejected a conversation or walked away from a situation that didn't support my goals and dreams and I felt feelings of guilt trying to make their way into my psyche. This is especially true when decisions you make effect others. Don't be tempted. Remember, guilt isn't allowed into the circle. After a short time, armed with the knowledge you've made a good decision that was in your best interest, those feelings of guilt go away and you begin to feel confident and content with your decision.

You have to consider yourself, your goals, your dreams, and your ambitions as sacred, as something to protect. The next time you're thinking about making a decision, big or small, whether it's changing jobs, moving, starting a business, having a baby, getting a dog - whatever it is - write it down in just a few words. Draw out the stick figure of yourself and then draw a circle around both. Just you and your vision. Hold it sacred. Protect it. And as life happens and negativity creeps in, write down all of the negative emotions that are presented to you throughout the day outside the circle. Don't give them any weight or merit yet. Don't give them any consideration at all. Just think of them as mini presentations that you'll decide whether to accept or reject at a later time. When the day is done, your mind is still and there's nothing pressing in your life, take some time to revisit the day's circle.

Remember, you and your vision inside the circle are all that matters. This is where you place all the power and all the focus. Give each negative word or phrase written outside the circle some consideration, and decide if you will allow it inside or not. It's very likely few will make the cut. If they don't, permanently delete them from your mind and don't give them a second thought, ever again. All that's left is you and your dream.... and that's all that matters.

TIGHTEN YOUR
INNER CIRCLE

TIGHTEN YOUR INNER CIRCLE

Wow, this was a tough one. For me, it was a tough transition going from the partying, high school and college days to a more focused adulthood. But it was far tougher transitioning to a life of total sobriety, living healthy, pursuing wellness and chasing my dreams. It was tough because a lot of relationships didn't survive the transition.

Growing up I forged a lot of really great friendships and, thankfully, there are still a couple alive and thriving today. Some... not so much. In many ways, my circle of friends were always the center of my universe. The thought of these people not being a part of my everyday life someday was absurd. We did everything together. We had endless fun together. We had everything in common. Of course we'd be friends forever... It's funny how goals and ambitions that are different from those around you reveal who your real friends are though.

How does one prepare for this? I'm not sure you do. Maybe we should first define friend. They say if you have just one true friend in life to count yourself lucky. I agree. To me a true friend is someone who is there, in your corner, unconditionally. One who accepts you just as you are, with all your bumps and bruises, and all your baggage. A true friend to me is one who feels safe telling you you're screwing up when your screwing up, and one who welcomes you to do the same, without fear of backlash or hurt feelings. Whether it's a time for laughing or for crying, each of you knows the other is always coming from a place of love.

From this perspective, looking back, I can see why many of the people in my life who I thought were my friends weren't really friends at all. But truthfully, I am forever grateful for all of the people who I've met and known in my life. They may not have turned out to be *true* friends but I consider them friends I was lucky enough to have known just the same. I'm thankful our paths crossed and the purpose they were meant to serve at the time was served, for both of us. Shouldn't this be the way we ought to be looking at it rather than looking back and remembering a person with anger or regret?

There are times when it is necessary to let people in your life go, even if you'd swear you were the best of friends. If a relationship with a friend or a significant other isn't peaceful and mutually supportive, tighten your inner circle. Be eternally grateful for having known that person when you did, and let them go. Know that the universe is just clearing a little space in your life for a true friend to show up.

People come into and out of our lives for a reason. The experience plays an important part in what makes us who we are today. Think about this a little deeper as you look back on your life. You can be eternally grateful for every single minute of your life, good and bad. Look at each memory with sincere joy and happiness because if just one minute of your life before today were any different, you wouldn't be standing where you are right now. This is an awesome notion. Life is an incredible journey. There are some seasons of life that are excruciating to go through. I've had my share. But it's a journey - and we have a lot of power within ourselves to see the glass as half full in any scenario.

GET OUT OF
YOUR COMFORT ZONE

GET OUT OF YOUR COMFORT ZONE

Get out of your comfort zone! We hear it all the time. Great motivators, sales coaches, mentors and self help gurus are forever telling us to get out of our comfort zone. Overall I think this is pretty good advice, to a point. Some of the best advice for beating self sabotage would certainly include getting outside, and staying outside, of your comfort zone. Meaningful, personal growth rarely occurs on the well-worn path of predictable habits. However, when it comes to beating self sabotage there is an essential caveat that should be included before venturing outside of your comfort zone. Build in escape routes.

Throwing caution to the wind is an awesome thing. It can be hugely beneficial when it comes to beating self sabotage. But when you're early in the process of developing strengths needed to overcome self sabotaging thoughts when they show up, it's very important to include strategies for relieving pressures that might build up while venturing in unfamiliar territory outside of your comfort zone. We want to maximize our efforts spent outside of our comfort zone without setting ourselves up for failure. After all, isn't our ultimate goal to form new habits, to realize personal growth, and to start living the lives we were meant to live? So why approach an opportunity to venture outside of our comfort zone - an opportunity that could get us one step closer to our ultimate goal - with blind and reckless abandon? It sounds good on paper but in practice it's a recipe for disaster.

Whether it's at work, with family members or with friends, most of us are usually people pleasers and are pretty quick to commit to all kinds of things that will help someone else. Once committed we are usually then trying to figure out how in the world we're going to pull off what we just committed to... either because we don't have the time or we don't have the skill set. The perception we have of our own abilities sometimes exceeds our actual abilities.

We might be temped to chalk these moments up as venturing outside of our comfort zone, like we're always told to do. But the pressures we put on ourselves in our quest to please others is often a prime ingredient for self sabotage. That sabotage then spills over into other areas of our life, and before we know it, we're right in the middle of a big problem that could have been totally avoidable.

I don't want to discourage good healthy adventures outside of your comfort zone. By all means, get outside and stay outside of your comfort zone, way outside of it in fact. But before you go be sure to build in strategies, which allow you to take the pressure off yourself along the way. In the next chapter I will share an awesome approach to this that I call chunk it down...

CHUNK IT DOWN

CHUNK IT DOWN

Very often we set goals with the end in mind. We forget about the journey. Setting more attainable "mini goals" or milestones to achieve during the journey towards our bigger goals and dreams not only serve as momentum builders but they can also serve as pressure relievers along the way.

There was a time during my pursuit of health and wellness when I was considering a big and scary goal for myself. So much had changed in my life. I couldn't believe how healthy I felt. I couldn't believe what size pants I was wearing. It was a bit euphoric and all I could think about was how I might share what I was learning with others. I became obsessed with the idea but I had no idea how to do it.

One of the DVD fitness programs that became my favorite was a cardio kickboxing program called Turbo Kick. I loved it! It was so fun and it was a great way to get my cardio in without boring myself to death on the treadmill. While researching the program further I came across some information online about the creator of the program. It turned out she was from my home state of Michigan and was offering certification classes all over the country which allowed certified instructors to actually teach Turbo Kick classes live. My husband suggested I look into getting certified and help people that way - through teaching group fitness classes.

The idea was exciting.... it was perfect! I imagined myself being a part of people's journey to fitness and wellness - really playing a role and being a mentor. I'd recently received my degree in psychology and had intended to become a substance abuse counselor. I always thought counseling would be a great fit for me anyway, so how perfect was this. I could share my passion for fitness, and connect with people on a personal level too. Then, all of a sudden, the thought of it scared me to death.

Teaching in front of people? Who was I to teach fitness? Who was I to counsel anyone? It wasn't that long ago when I was hungover and borderline morbidly obese... who would even come to my classes? Self sabotage started to creep in to my thoughts... but why? I had just accomplished some pretty hefty goals I'd set for myself. I was sober. I quit smoking. I lost 50 pounds. I was healthy and fit for the first time in my life, plus I had a burning desire to help people. It seemed like I should have all the confidence in the world. But self sabotage managed to take hold once again. I'm a little embarrassed to admit it now but I lamented over the decision to become certified to teach Turbo Kick classes for two whole years. For two years I made excuses, procrastinated, lived in fear, doubted myself, hid under the covers and buried my head in the sand. Two whole years were wasted.

The big scary goal for me was teaching in front of a class full of people. But I didn't have a class full of people... I didn't even have a job at a gym that would allow me to teach in front of a class full of people. In fact, I wasn't even certified to teach in the first place so what was I so immediately scared of? That thought process convinced me I wasn't going to waste another two years. But I had to figure out a way to work towards my goal of teaching without putting a lot of pressure on myself. So I decided to chunk it down.

Chunk it down is a process of creating intermittent "psychologically soothing" exit ramps on the road to reaching a big scary goal. This may sound a little strange at first, but stay with me. This is one of the most powerful self sabotage busters I've found yet for reaching a goal!

To overcome the intense fear and doubt I'd had about teaching group exercise classes in front of a bunch of people I don't know, I had to first stop the inner monologue of endless excuses that always ended with a no, and begin a conversation with myself that started with a *conditional* yes. Here's how it went.

"Yes, I will sign up for certification classes and go to California for testing. I'm just signing up though. This doesn't mean I have to actually go inside and take the class. All I have to do is take a nice trip to California, enjoy some new scenery, and if I decide to go through with certification, I will." Psychologically soothing exit strategy #1 - and one step closer to my goal. No pressure.

The conversation continues... "So now I'm here in California, feeling great. The gym looks nice, the people look nice. I've come this far... why not. I'll just go in and take the certification classes. It'll be fun. It doesn't mean I have to actually teach any classes. I'll just be certified to teach just in case I choose to teach, sometime later in life." Psychologically soothing exit strategy #2 - and one more step closer to my goal. No pressure.

The conversation continues... "Wow, that was fun! I actually did it! I'm actually certified to be a group fitness instructor. With newfound confidence, I'm going to go back home and apply at a few gyms, just to see if I can get an audition to actually become an instructor. This doesn't mean I have to actually take the job if I'm offered one, I just want to see if I get offered a class to teach." Psychologically soothing exit strategy #3 - and one more step closer to my goal. No pressure.

You see where I'm going with this. I took baby steps towards my goal and always allowed myself an out. This drastically reduced pressures I was feeling from the scarier big picture. The inner monologue I was used to having with myself, was very different now. Instead of beating myself up with fears and doubts looking at the big picture, I just started allowing room for the possibility of achieving smaller, mini goals along the way. By the time I got to a place where I was actually auditioning for teaching positions, I was so confident I actually decided to turn down a couple offers until the one that fit me best came along. As silly as it sounds, this exercise is extremely powerful to start the process of changing habits. The more you do it, the easier it gets. Before you know it, new habits are fully formed. Taking on new challenges is not only not a problem any more, you begin to seek out new challenges. In fact, new challenges begin to seek you out, doors start opening up, and the world starts to look like a whole new place.

Since becoming a group fitness instructor I've also become an ACE certified personal trainer. With five full group fitness classes every week, and a growing personal training client list, I have the opportunity every day to help people change their bodies and change their minds through fitness and wellness. The feeling is indescribable. I often wonder - what if I had totally surrendered to the thoughts I was having about not being good enough, not having

what it takes to be an instructor, that no one would
even come to my classes....

The universe needs us to step out of our comfort
zones, WAY out. Set big scary goals. But rather than
look at your goals as one big goal, chunk them
down into little, manageable goals and build in
psychologically soothing exit strategies. You have
nothing to lose.

SHOOT FOR THE MIDDLE

SHOOT FOR THE MIDDLE

Taking a new approach to getting where I wanted to
go, managing expectations, and adopting a new
perspective of what excellence really means for me,
were all critical steps in my process of beating self
sabotage.

We live in a society and a social structure that
demands more, bigger, better, taller, higher, farther,
excellence, constant improvement and even
perfection (whatever that is). We are constantly
bombarded with the imagery of what "perfect
people" are supposed to look like and what people
who have "made it" are supposed to act like. Turn
on the TV or surf the Internet and you'll see a
never-ending stream of who the "winners" are and
how they're *living their best lives now.*" It's
nauseating.

First one in, last one out, body fat percentages,
calories, the right car, the right neighborhood, the

right job, the right friends, the right church, the right clothes, Facebook, iPhones, instant messaging, constant contact.... it never ends. How do we keep up? How do we even know what the right thing to think is anymore? What fits the upwardly mobile aspiration mold of the power players of the world? And what am I doing wrong!? It seems that all of this excellence messaging has been building momentum at a frightening pace over the past decade. Could life get any crazier? Much like all of the negative global fallout following the burst of the real estate bubble in 2008, will the excellence movement of this hyper society be the next bubble that's going to burst? Are we all going to self implode when it does? O.k. maybe that was a little much.... but this whole bigger better faster thing is getting out of control.

The "pressure to perform" in this modern world became too much for me one day. So I decided I was going to let myself off the hook and I took myself out of the game... so to speak. I decided I was going to approach this excellence thing from a slightly different angle. Instead of every day being a "game changing" opportunity to take it to the top, I decided I was going to "shoot for the middle!"

My friend Amanda shared this concept with me and I have to admit, at first it sounded a little silly. We're always told to shoot for the top! Go for it! Reach for the brass ring! Go big or go home! So how does aiming for the middle make any sense at all, and why would someone make it their goal? The premise behind shoot for the middle is very simple - *Master the middle and the top will come to you.*

I love that! And in practice it has proven to be so true! When pursuing a goal or a dream, put all of your focus and energy on mastering the basics. Set some interim, attainable goals. Register a few victories and build some momentum on your way to mastering the middle. Think of it like putting to a bigger hole. In putting, the goal is to get the ball in the cup. In simple terms, that's the goal, that's the victory, that's the brass ring. When you're on the green, and you're staring down a 20 foot put, it's a proven fact that a higher percentage of golfers sink that put when they visualize the hole being bigger than it actually is. The ultimate goal is to sink the put. But the immediate objective is to hit the bigger hole you see around the actual hole. Don't try to put the ball in the smaller hole (shoot for the top) put the ball in the bigger hole (shoot for the middle) and you'll likely sink the put (the top will come to you).

The objective is to identify goals and dreams for our lives and to then pursue and reach them. For those of us who battle through feelings of fear, doubt and guilt this is a difficult process. As a matter of fact, even if you aren't one who battles through self sabotaging thoughts in pursuit of a dream, setting and reaching goals is almost never an easy undertaking. Are you familiar with the 80/20 rule? The actual name for the 80/20 rule is the Pareto principle. It suggests that about 80% of the effects of any endeavor come from about 20% of the causes. It's a common rule of thumb measurement that can be applied fairly accurately to most anything. For example, 80% of a country's wealth is controlled by 20% of its population. The problem with many who fall into the 80% category is that they set their immediate goal as being among the 20%. If they would set their sites on being the master of the 80%, being counted among the 20% will come to them.

Let me give you an example. Trainers in the gym are typically a very competitive group of people, and the 80/20 rule applies among them. 80% of the clients, who use a personal trainer at the gym, train with 20% of the trainers. And with 20% of the trainers getting 80% of the clients, guess who's battling for the remaining 20% of the clients - 80% of the trainers. Pretty typical. If a new trainer were to apply the modern life excellence principles of shooting for the top and reaching for the brass ring, naturally their objective would be to get into that

20% group as quickly as possible. A different approach for this new trainer though would be to forget all about the 20% and focus on becoming the master of the 80%. Sweat the small stuff, train a little harder, show up a little earlier and stay a little longer. Without all of the pressures of competing amongst those high achievers in the 20% club, being a shining beacon amongst the 80% group becomes the only objective. Having totally mastered the middle, pretty soon the top will come a calling.

We all dream of doing big things with our lives. Whatever your vocation or pursuit, there are usually those in the group that seem to excel and there are those who don't ever seem to get too far off the ground. Those who are floundering around in the 80% group usually spend a lot of time beating themselves up, focusing on what people are doing at the top. Don't. It's a trap of self sabotage that's hard to get out of. Instead, shoot for the middle.

Take the pressure off. The middle is doable; you can see it a little more clearly.

For me, I recognized my little car was perfect, my little apartment was perfect, I loved my job, I loved myself, and from now on I was going to stop playing into all the hype of what I thought the world expected of me and I was going to be happy just being me. That didn't mean I was lowering the bar for myself. Not at all. I simply decided I was going to dictate the terms of how I was going to get to where I wanted to go. I decided I would still aspire to the same lofty goals I'd set for myself, but I was going to drastically simplify my approach to getting there.

Outside of the lofty goals and dreams we set for ourselves in our own personal lives, shooting for the middle in the everyday stuff yields enormously positive results as well. Take the time to open a door for someone, drop some change in the cup of a charitable cause, volunteer, listen, slow down on your way to work, take a walk instead of watching TV, do a favor for someone without expecting anything in return, acquiesce during a disagreement, say your sorry, master the small things in life.

It seems like we're all waiting for those big A' Ha! moments, the breakthroughs, the game changers. What we often forget is there are a whole lot of little victories on the road to the championship ring. Master the basics, relish in the simple steps along the way. Savor every one of them. View all of the small things as big ones because in truth, they really are... Tomorrow isn't guaranteed.

GET MOVING!
KEEP MOVING!

GET MOVING! KEEP MOVING!

Thoughtful contemplation on most any subject can be a good thing. In the context of procrastination, which is one of the main contributing factors leading to self sabotage, contemplation is crippling. It has been said that action is the enemy of thought. I couldn't agree more. So I say, take action! Get moving, and keep moving! When I embarked on my mission of positive change six years ago I can't tell you how many times I found myself embroiled in a mind numbing conversation in my head with myself about whether or not I could or should do this or that. Hundreds, thousands maybe. If I weren't so thankful for every moment of my life that has led me to this very moment, I might be tempted to be really mad at all the time I wasted over-thinking just about everything I ever wanted to do.

Think about this statement carefully - *action is the enemy of thought*. Should you ever find yourself deliberating and debating with yourself about the merits of some leap you're considering taking in your quest for forward momentum, let me offer you the following... Stop thinking! Get moving! Keep moving!

Some of the biggest A'ha! moments I've ever experienced were when I would stop thinking about taking steps towards a goal and would actually take steps toward it. There were times when I would labor and dread over a decision for years. Years! Once action had actually been taken though - rarely, if ever, did any of the fears or doubts I was endlessly contemplating in my mind ever come true. There were definitely times when I stumbled and fell in the course of taking action. But any fallout that resulted from the stumble or fall was so inconsequential; it barely registered in the whole scheme of things anyway. None of my doubts or fears ever came true. Conversely, the little slivers of positivity that managed to work there way into the conversations I was having with myself seemed to always come true though. Funny how that works...

Make it a priority every single day to take action steps towards your goals, whether they're big or small. And never use your perception of someone else's life - whether it's someone in your everyday life or some media figure - as a gauge from which to measure your own progress or success. It's absolutely incredible to me how the media, with scientific advertising algorithms, marketing schemes, and branding methods, paint an unattainable, fairy tale picture of what real success is supposed to look like or what pretty people are supposed to look like. There have been many times on my journey when I felt pretty darn good about how I was feeling, how I was looking, and about the progress I was making towards my goals, when I would get sucked in to some clever messaging from a well placed ad about what feeling good and looking good was supposed to look like. It would totally derail any positive imagery I was enjoying about myself that day. Free yourself from this illusion once and for all.

Until I started measuring my own success and my own progress from factual information I had about myself from the week before, I thought my efforts were a waste of time. If last week I did five push ups, and this week I did six, progress! Success! Who cares if someone else can do 100 push-ups. The bottom line is this - this is your world, your life, and no one else's. Success and progress in your life can only be measured by you and is irrelevant when compared to anyone else's. Get up, get moving, and keep moving towards your own dreams. And don't forget to savor every minute along the way.

THE REAL SECRET

THE REAL SECRET

It is my sincere belief that my soul's purpose in this life is to help people help themselves. The most impactful way I know to achieve this is to show people how to get out of their own way. We are our own worst enemy most of the time. It's not our fault though. It's becoming increasingly harder and harder to avoid. We live in the information age and there is clearly no shortage of information coming at us non-stop, and from all directions. We also live in a time where everything, and I mean everything, is processed or engineered, including thoughts. It seems as though there's a newer or better way to think about or do whatever it is we happen to be thinking or doing at the time. The new normal. A new paradigm. These are just illusions and the more of the world's illusions that we pack into our brains and bodies, the more susceptible we are to falling victim to self sabotage.

The purpose of this book is to share with you the most effective, tried and true strategies I've taken over the past six years to beat self sabotage. I've tried to leave out the fluff as best I could. In order to build a strong foundation for successfully beating self sabotage I believe each step in this process, as they're laid out, is critically important. But I believe this final step is by far the most important step of all. All the other steps serve an important purpose. We have to be able to look in the mirror and see our true selves. We have to purge the junk. We have to free ourselves from the illusions that have held us prisoner. We have to develop strategies that help us begin a journey down a path towards realizing our goals and dreams. But the message of this chapter is one that, if enthusiastically practiced daily, will not only keep self sabotage at bay for good, it will also free us completely, allowing us to truly live the life we were meant to live.

In this final step I invite you to now shift the focus of your efforts and the focus of your energies away from yourself and place them onto others. You've all heard about The Secret? This is the *real* secret.

There is no more useful or greater sustainable therapy on earth than loving others more than you love yourself, or helping others before you help yourself, or giving to others before you give to yourself, without expectation. Contrary to the popular notion *pay yourself first* - paying others first is a far more impactful strategy for living the good life. I'm not suggesting you break out your checkbook and start handing out money. I'm talking about loving others and helping others through the giving of your heart, your spirit, and your time.

Think about a special joy you felt at some point in your life, or you're feeling now, that might be transferrable to someone else who needs it. Maybe a special music instructor taught you to play the piano. You can pay that joy forward by giving a little time each week or each month in a nursing home, playing piano for the residents there. You'd make their day beyond words and you'd permanently imprint an even deeper joy into your own soul in the process. Maybe you were overweight, sick, and tired, and a trainer helped you to lose weight and feel better than you've ever felt. Pay that feeling of wellness forward by volunteering to organize a fitness class at your local YMCA, maybe even teach it. You will forever change people's lives and you will play an active part in making the world a better place.

Opportunities to love, help and give are all around us constantly. It's easy to do, and requires little to no sacrifice at all. It's also contagious. Anonymous giving is always best. Let your light shine and people will just see something different in you. The positive aura and positive energy you emit will attract others and will prompt others to do the same.

However you choose to give of yourself in your community or in your family is up to you. But start to program your mind to look for opportunities to give of yourself in some small way every day. You may just offer warm eye contact with someone, or you may give a smile to someone you might normally avoid. Giving without expectation changes our hearts and changes the world. There is never a reason to be angry or be in a hurry. If you feel your blood start to boil over something, remember the circle. Step back and analyze the cost of the anger before you get mad. If you're running late, be late. Slow down and experience every step you take and every moment you're given. Remember, tomorrow isn't guaranteed. Today is the best time to live... so live now!

.....Love Erica

HOW I BEAT SELF SABOTAGE AND HOW YOU CAN TOO

Erica Snyder

Gypsy Publishers